ARCTIC

Music, Images & CD-ROM from the Northwest Passage

ODYSSEY

Richard Olsenius

BLUESTEM PRODUCTIONS

Published by Bluestem Productions, Box 381, Annapolis, MD 21404
Printed in the United States of America

http://www.ArcticOdyssey.com
Bluestem@BluestemMedia.com

Library of Congress Catalog Card Number: 98-96817

ISBN 0-9609064-9-5

FIRST EDITION, 1998   10 9 8 7 6 5 4 3 2 1

I think over again...my small adventures, my fears, those small ones that seem so big. I had to get and to reach and yet, there is only one Great Thing...The only thing is to live and to see the great day that dawns and the light that fills the world.

— OLD INUIT SONG

This book, music and

CD-ROM are dedicated to

those who have come

before, through this harsh

yet beautiful land, and to

those who now live along

one of the last true

wilderness areas of this

small planet.

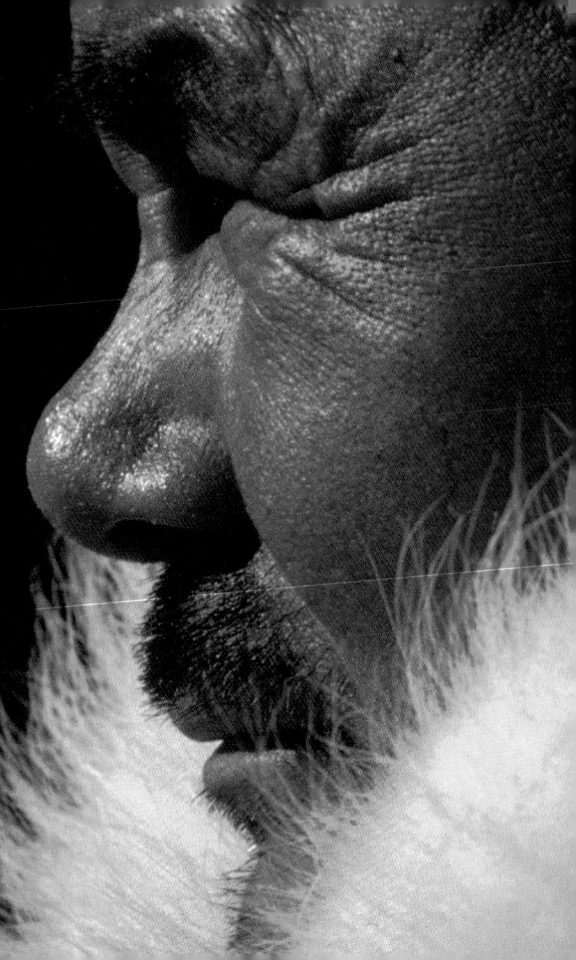

CONTENTS

I. THE VOYAGE OF THE BELVEDERE

My first introduction to the Arctic was by plane. As I flew north from my home in Minnesota, I watched farmland yield to endless miles of black spruce—the taiga of Canada. Beyond Yellowknife in the Northwest Territories, the landscape slowly lost its thick cover of trees, giving way to the vast and unspoiled arctic wilderness. As the plane descended toward Victoria Island, I could see the small town of Cambridge Bay and the 60-foot yacht *Belvedere*, which would be my home for the next two months on a voyage through the Northwest Passage.

Belvedere's captain, John Bockstoce, was making his sixth attempt to sail the Arctic coast of North America from Alaska to Greenland, hoping to pilot the first American yacht through the Northwest Passage. For the last five summers ice had blocked his way, forcing him to turn back and store *Belvedere* in an arctic port each winter. But this year Bockstoce, an expert in arctic whaling and Inuit culture, hoped it would be different. Sailing the entire Northwest Passage was his dream.

Stretching 3,500 miles from the Bering Sea on the west coast of Alaska to Davis Strait on the east coast of Baffin Island, the Northwest Passage has long been a highway of change. Ancient nomadic hunters stalked game along its shores. European explorers searched in vain for a shortcut to the Orient. Today geologists prospect here for oil and gas deposits and scientists search for new information on the environment. Waterways and land forms bear the names of many of those early adventurers—Baffin, Banks, Barrow, Bellot, Peary, and many others.

Hundreds have lost their lives searching for a route through these treacherous waters. The most famous was the Sir John Franklin expedition of 1845-47, when 129 men perished. Though more than 40 rescue expeditions were launched, neither ships nor men were ever found. The Northwest Passage was not successfully navigated until a Norwegian explorer, Roald Amundsen, threaded his 70-foot herring sloop through the maze of icy channels and bays in the early 1900's. Since then, fewer than 50 vessels (mostly military ships) have traversed the Northwest Passage, and no American yacht had successfully made the journey. From the deck of a small ship like *Belvedere*, it was easy to see why; shifting ice floes, shoals and rocks, poor charts, and little chance of rescue if a problem arose.

For nearly 40 days we picked our way through one of the world's last expanses of wilderness, home to seabirds, musk oxen, seals, arctic foxes, and polar bears. I was overwhelmed by the quantity and diversity of wildlife. This narrow arctic waterway provided food for wildlife while the surrounding coast provided a safe breeding ground for waterfowl. We marked each whale siting in our ship's log. Apart from the wildlife, there was little human contact. We bought supplies at a handful of Inuit villages along the Passage, but for the most part it was like sailing from New York to London with only five towns in between.

Through much of August the days blended into one another as we cruised along the low, rocky coast east of Cambridge Bay. On the horizon we occasionally saw cairns—stone obelisks raised by ancient hunters for navigation or channeling caribou for ambush.

It was at our anchorage near the James Ross Strait on the eastern side of the Canadian Arctic, when the weather we feared most caught up with us. We had taken time to explore the shoreline, building a cairn in memory of our voyage. That night the ice shifted and large chunks floated into our bay, bringing their own fog bank in tow. There was a frantic effort to weigh anchor, but the fast-moving ice trapped the *Belvedere*. For three days we felt the confines of the boat. A trip to the deck and a view of the icebound universe surrounding us only intensified the feeling of helplessness. I couldn't help but think of early explorers and so many failed expeditions.

On the fourth day a strong easterly wind moved the pack ice in our favor, opening a narrow channel north to Bellot Strait. If the ice moved back, *Belvedere* would be pushed up on shore. But the wind held until we reached Bellot Strait, the 15-mile-long channel between Somerset Island and the Boothia Peninsula. Here tides of the eastern Arctic meet those of the west. Barely a quarter-mile wide in some places with 7-to-13-knot tidal currents, Bellot Strait cuts across the northernmost tip of North America. We waited for the rushing tide to ebb, then quickly motored between the rocky cliffs, through our last great obstacle along the Northwest Passage. That

night we sailed through a thin sheet of new ice, listening to the distant sounds of bowhead whales.

To the east of Bellot Strait the arctic landscape becomes more mountainous and majestic, like the Rocky Mountains rising up from the prairies. After sailing around Brodeur Peninsula, we made our way toward Baffin Island. It is the world's fifth largest island and claims the world's longest fjords and highest sheer-faced cliffs. The glaciated mountains of nearby Bylot Island are equally breathtaking. Protected as a wildlife sanctuary, the island provides breeding ground for millions of waterfowl, and marine mammals.

As we traced the rugged western coast of Baffin Island, an early winter storm drove snow and freezing rain into our faces. We ducked into a fjord to wait it out. Even though *Belvedere* was less than 30-feet from shore, the anchor never touched bottom: the fathometer showed the depth at 900 feet. As the wind howled, we spent the night motoring to keep *Belvedere* off the shore.

To reach our final destination, we had to leave the picturesque town of Pond Inlet on Baffin Island and cross 300 miles of "iceberg alley"—Davis Strait. Through this corridor icebergs calved from Greenland's glaciers pass on their migration to the North Atlantic. Wind and waves have sculpted these floating islands, some as large as aircraft carriers, into an endless variety of shapes. As I looked at each passing iceberg, it was hard to fathom that four-fifths of its total mass lay underwater. We gave them a wide berth, as they can roll over without warning and create a dangerous surge.

On our final leg to Greenland we kept a 24-hour watch for icebergs and the dangerous "growlers," large chunks of barely visible ice that have broken off from the main icebergs. But after three days of nearly flat calm, *Belvedere* motored out of an early morning fog into Sisimiut Harbor, completing its long, historic voyage to become the first American yacht to traverse the Northwest Passage.

The Arctic holds a fascination for many people. It is that final frontier where explorers have wanted to leave their mark, but in the end the Arctic leaves its imprint on us. It is a place not to be conquered but to be experienced. The crew of the *Belvedere* were each changed in the process of this voyage. For me, the Arctic spoke to a need for open spaces, adventure and wilderness. It offered me an opportunity to experience something so powerful and majestic, that it forever changed my perception of my life and my world.

II. JOURNEY TO THE WATERSKY

The 24-hour daylight of the arctic summer gave a surrealistic feeling to normal activities and threw off my sense of timing. The sounds of Inuit children playing kickball at 3 a.m. disrupted my sleep. Yet the best light of the day for photography was the four to five hours of extended twilight after midnight when the low sun drew out the colors of the landscape. It was also the safest time to travel on the melting, shifting ice. Most Inuit hunting parties traveled in these early morning hours. It was eerie to be skimming across the ice on snowmobiles with the sun still hitting the peaks of glaciers.

Experienced hunters can discern open water from a distance because it reflects less light onto the underside of low-lying clouds than ice, creating a dark band. The Inuit call this shadow "water-sky." Traveling to the "water-sky" or floe edge was grueling, for endless pressure ridges and deep pools of melting water made progress slow and bone jarring.

We seemed to be snowmobiling on water: the meltwater lay on top of the ice like an endless lake. To cross the leads of open water, we had to plane the snowmobiles across them at high speeds. I tried not to peer down into the leads, which could be 15-feet wide. The water looked black, its depth indecipherable. Hunters follow these leads because they are the pathways for their prey—seals, narwhals, belugas, and bowhead whales.

In spring and summer the ice is a living, breathing membrane that constantly moans, cracks, and shifts. It can never be trusted. On one hunting trip we rode 30 miles into Baffin Bay and set up camp at the floe edge. We were awakened at 3 a.m. by the shouts of a hunter who noticed that our camp was drifting out to sea. We used our snowmobiles to plane over the expanding lead and reach the safety of land-fast ice. Waking from a sound sleep to

race the shifting ice gave me new respect for the ever present dangers of working and traveling in this raw land.

One morning I took a helicopter to the floe edge. From the air I saw pods of narwhals and belugas working their way along the dark leads veining the ice. How did they know which leads were open and which were dead ends? Even Inuit hunters marveled at their ability to navigate through icebound arctic waters.

We touched down just 50-feet from open water and bounced the helicopter skids on the ice several times to make sure it was strong enough to hold our weight. I climbed out and felt as though I were standing on the edge of world. The mountains were coated in white, and the sky was bathed in blue-gray with a touch of mauve. White chunks of ice flecked the green-blue ocean. I listened to the deep sighs of the narwhals as they surfaced for air, their spiral tusks lifting gracefully from the water. I could see the white iridescence of belugas swimming beneath them. Nearby, hundreds of eiders were taking off and landing. I will never forget the intimacy I felt toward the Arctic in that early morning twilight on the floe edge.

Ice defines the Arctic. It determines the type and timing of activities along the coast, from navigation to the migration of whales. A good percentage of the Inuit vocabulary relates to the condition of sea ice and techniques for traveling and hunting on it.

By cooling the warmer air circulating north from the tropics, arctic ice even plays an important role in regulating the global climate. If environmental changes were to alter the Arctic's ability to regulate these temperatures, weather patterns and sea levels could change around the world.

The warm air circulating north and east to the Arctic regions carries organic pollutants and heavy metals deep into the polar environment. These toxic substances do not break down easily in the cold temperatures and low sunlight of the Arctic. They accumulate in the fat of fish and marine mammals, ultimately threatening the health of the Inuit, whose diet is rich in food from the sea.

I was continually reminded that while the Arctic is geographically remote, it is still irrevocably linked with communities thousands of miles away.

III. HUNTERS OF THE FLOE EDGE

I arrived in Barrow, Alaska, when the spring bowhead whale hunt is usually at its peak. It was early May, the time when these huge marine mammals migrate northeast along the low-lying coast toward Banks Island. Bowheads have an uncanny ability to follow shoreline leads, yet therein lies their vulnerability. These narrow channels through the ice also make it easier for Inupiat (Alaska Eskimo) hunters to locate their prey. But nature has a way of evening the odds: this year strong northerly winds had kept the shoreline leads closed.

"The leads have never been closed off by ice like this before," said wildlife manager Craig George as he prepared to go out on his snowmobile to check the ice. "There certainly won't be many whales harvested with conditions like this."

Craig has spent the last ten years keeping track of whale populations for the North Slope Borough, which is part of the Alaskan land settlement claim for native people. When a whale is harvested, a team from Barrow measures, weighs, and collects samples of the whale. The North Slope Borough has hired specialists like George as part of a management plan to preserve hunting as a way of life for the native peoples of the Arctic.

Barrow, which faces the Chukchi Sea, is the northernmost city in the United States and a western outpost along the Northwest Passage. It lives up to its reputation as a tough whaling community.

Some of the Inupiat whaling crews had moved far out on the ice, while others waited in town, hoping the leads would open closer to shore. As the days passed, it became obvious that the seasonal quota for bowheads would not be met by the village.

But ice conditions are not the only challenge. In 1977 Alaska banned whale hunting. It resumed two years later after the Alaska native community reached an agreement with the

International Whaling Commission (IWC). In the meantime, animosity grew in Barrow over what the natives felt was interference by southerners in their traditional way of life. They viewed the ban as one more effort to force assimilation into the white man's culture—even though wildlife biologists had confirmed that the bowhead population in the western Arctic was healthy and growing.

I had been waiting in Barrow for two weeks to join a whaling crew, but with the terrible ice conditions I doubted I would have a chance. Suddenly the phone rang late one afternoon, and an hour later I was standing on the back of a wooden sled called a komatik, pulled along the shore of the Chukchi Sea at 30-miles an hour by Craig's snowmobile. It was well below freezing, and the windchill was numbing my hands. But the exhilaration of gliding along the frozen ocean, dodging car-size chunks of ice and deep pools of water, flying over pressure ridges and then slamming down, made me forget about the temperature.

By now dozens of snowmobiles had overtaken us. I felt a growing sense of security when I realized that the entire village of Barrow seemed to be heading to the floe edge—the dangerous, shifting line where land-fast ice meets open water. I now understood what a whale hunt means to a community. This chase, in one

form or another, had been played out for many generations, yet I wondered how the early Eskimo managed without the snowmobile.

By 9 p.m. we had reached the sliver of open water extending from a larger lead some distance off. The whaling captain, who provides the boats and supplies for a team of eight or so men, was standing alongside the lead, watching for his crew to return.

"I'm proud of my crew," he said. "They got the whale with one shot, and soon we will have it up there on the ice." He was pleased to have taken Barrow's first whale of the season. The whaling captain called to the crowd, "We need pullers. Come on, haul." Others chimed in, "Carry on back . . . keep pulling . . . haul away." By now a hundred people were pulling on the inch-thick line attached to the tail. "Harder now," someone yelled.

Suddenly, from behind my back, I heard what sounded like a shotgun blast as the broken line shot past me. Like a line of dominoes, people fell into the snow, their hands stung by the snapped line. The bowhead slid back into the water. Luckily no one was seriously hurt and the process of raising the 50-ton whale began again.

By 4 a.m. the great dark hulk was out of the water. There would be plenty of meat and muktuk (skin and blubber) for all. For the next six hours, men with cutters sectioned the whale. Others dragged the hunks, one by one, away from the carcass to cool. Craig George and his crew were busy measuring and weighing pieces of the whale. "We hope to better understand the bowhead and what it weighs in relation to its size," he said as he and an assistant weighed a hunk of meat.

Nearly 12 hours later the carcass had been stripped clean and left for the polar bears. Exhausted families loaded up their share of meat and muktuk for the three-hour trip back to Barrow. Some remained to hunt seals and polar bears. As I stood on the back of the sled for the long ride back, I wondered how many more years this tradition would continue.

SOME 2,000 MILES TO THE EAST, SNOWMOBILES AND SLEDS were parked along the icy shore of Pond Inlet, like cars in a shopping center lot. It was July—summer in the Arctic—and the ice had begun to melt. Pond Inlet is a small village at the northern tip of Baffin Island in the eastern Canadian Arctic.

Each summer hunters pack their snowmobiles for a journey to the floe edge of Baffin Bay to hunt the narwhal. Our trip would take at least two weeks, but with round-the-clock sunshine weakening the ice, no one knew how long the ice would be safe for

travel. Many hunters had already returned, afraid of being stranded on a shifting ice flow.

Leo Muktar, my guide, paused as he rowed us across the open meltwater to his snowmobile. The late afternoon sun painted his face a deep yellow. "There are four corners to this world," he said softly, "and this place is one of them." When he was not hunting or fishing, activities he clearly preferred, Leo drove a taxi in the village.

"We have to travel during the evening," said Levi Koman-gapik with a grin that worried me. "There is so much meltwater already on the ice that we need to take advantage of a low sun and cooler temperatures." Levi is a friend of Leo's and a member of the hunting group.

"You have to remember that there is still four feet of ice under you," said Leo. "It is only the freshwater that is melting and sitting on the surface." That was soon apparent when we stopped for tea and scooped water from a pool. It was clear and sweet.

Even though Inuit hunters have spent their lives traversing this terrain, I felt apprehensive about riding 30 miles across melting ice on a machine not built for the pounding of ice ridges and constant drenching in shallow meltwater. With no weather reports and little chance of immediate help, I wondered if we were all insane. If a strong wind broke off the ice shelf you were camped on, you could only watch—and hope you could radio for help. What if the weather closed in? What if the ice started to break up? I now understood why the hunters had aluminum boats strapped to their komatiks.

As we traveled through the night to take advantage of cooler temperatures and the low "midnight sun," we stopped every hour for tea and pilot biscuits. Those round, almost tasteless crackers have sustained northern travelers for years. About 2 a.m., we approached our first lead.

Only 10 to 15-feet wide, these early leads were easily crossed . . . if you knew what you were doing. The hunter unhooked the komatik and left it on one side of the crack, then ran the snowmobile across, hooked up a long line to the komatik, and pulled it across with a quick surge of power. The objective was to keep everything dry and not have to pull the heavy sled back up on the ice. But the leads became wider and the process trickier. Hours later we reached the last lead just shy of the open ocean.

"This is the one we have to watch," Leo said as he looked for a good place to cross. "This is the ice that can move on us if the wind blows or the currents carry it out." As I watched the hunters'

faces, I could tell that everyone's senses were heightened. Here we were, 30 miles out in Baffin Bay, connected to land by only a thin skin of ice.

I walked off alone to photograph the floe edge, when suddenly the ice gave way and I was up to my neck in freezing water. My first reaction was not panic but to try and pull myself out of the water. I could feel the water filling my boots and wind pants and finally reaching my chest. I instinctively clutched my cameras with one hand and grabbed for what I thought was firm ice with the other, but my hand grasped only slush. Desperately I reached out again, only to realize that with the weight of cameras and water-soaked clothing, I was losing buoyancy. I could now feel the stinging cold of the water.

As I shouted for help, I could barely see the hunter named Thomas just a hundred yards away. It took him a few seconds to realize what had happened as he looked back unable to see me. Thomas usually moved slowly and deliberately, but now he bounded toward me, aware that my situation was perilous. His words came to me slowly and clearly, in a strong Inuit accent. "Hold yur han like dis," he said as he stretched out his cupped hand. With wet, cold hands it is difficult to pull a person to safety, so we cupped our fingers together in a solid grip, like a rail car coupling, and he hauled me up on the ice.

It was not long before I was in a tent, stripping off wet clothes and putting on a spare set of dry ones. For years I had carried spare clothing, always wondering if it was worth the weight and effort. This one time made it all worthwhile. An hour later I was back with the hunters, looking for narwhals along the floe edge.

"Listen. Did you hear that?" asked Levi as a deep whooshing sound echoed across the ice. "Narwhals."

We could hear the almost human-like breathing of two or three distant narwhals as they moved unseen in the ice rubble. As the small whales passed nearby, I watched the hunters stand a silent vigil along the floe edge. Their forms were outlined in the soft yellow glow of morning light. Like their ancestors before them, they were part of a long tradition of subsistence hunters whose skills were essential to their community's survival. I surveyed the icebound expanse and remembered Leo's words: "There are four corners to the world, and this place is one of them."

IV. THE NEW EXPLORERS

Surprisingly little was known about the Arctic until well into the 20th century. There were still areas that had never been mapped, weather phenomena that were not understood, and wildlife that had never been monitored. The Second World War highlighted the strategic importance of the Arctic as a fragile barrier between North America and Eurasia. The war years generated a great deal of information about weather, aviation, and navigation in the far North. The data on weather forecasting proved so valuable that Canada and the United States agreed to build five weather stations on the Queen Elizabeth Islands.

The Cold War furthered the Arctic's strategic position between the Soviet Union and the United States. As Soviet bombers developed the capability of reaching American targets via the Arctic, the United States and Canada built a chain of radar stations stretching from Greenland to Alaska called the Distant Early Warning (DEW) line. Most of the stations were built along the routes of the Northwest Passage where supply ships could reach them.

Scientific exploration offered the Canadian government a way to achieve a greater presence in the region and to expand knowledge of the resource base. The data that Canadian researchers gathered was crucial to oil and gas development, determining the effects of year-round navigation of the Passage and understanding the life cycle and health of wildlife populations.

I saw great determination in the modern-day explorers I met along the Northwest Passage. They seemed to reflect the same curiosity and commitment to discovering the secrets of the Arctic as earlier explorers. Scientists worked under difficult weather conditions at remote research sites, sometimes hundreds of miles from medical facilities or rescue operations. Seismic crews from Canada and the United States crisscrossed the landscape, prospecting for oil and gas deposits to meet growing energy demands. From the air, their grids scarred the tundra like an intricate game of tic-tac-toe.

I wondered how energy development might affect the delicate tundra, wildlife and native communities? Tanker traffic and any oil spills would have a major impact on whales and other sea life along the Passage. With the Arctic becoming a battleground between preservationists and developers, expanding our knowledge of the arctic environment is vital to protecting this fragile land.

On a cold morning in late winter I climbed into a helicopter for a ride from Resolute to a polynya research site on Little Cornwallis Island, where scientists were studying walruses and polar bears. The wind had continued to build as we left Resolute. Eventually, the pilot spotted a small shack perched on the edge of a cliff overlooking a polynya—a section of open water in the sea ice. Landing on the uneven terrain was tricky, and in the time it took me to remove my camera bags and duffel, the pilot was already lifting off. Social amenities are brief when the weather is deteriorating.

Through the afternoon the wind continued to build to gale force. One of the caps even blew off the camp's anemometer, which measures wind speed. In the dusky twilight, rich with shades of blue and purple, the temperature dipped to 30°F below zero.

Polynyas play an important role in the arctic food chain. Like oases in a desert of ice, they stay open all year due to a mixing of ocean currents which bring krill, plankton and and other important food for wildlife. Since 1980 Canadian researchers have been documenting the marine mammals living in this polynya. There is concern that shipping in this area may impact the walrus and polar bear populations, already in a precarious balance. Through a hydrophone (underwater microphone) I could hear the unique clicking sounds of the walruses. I was amazed how this distant world of water and ice was filled with life.

From Little Cornwallis Island I flew to a remote location on Victoria Island with Dr. Mitch Taylor and wildlife manager Randall Glaholt, Canadian researchers who were putting satellite-tracking collars on adult polar bears. Concerned about the viability of these great white bears, the largest land carnivore, Taylor and Glaholt have been studying their population, health, and movements.

Shortly after I arrived, the weather closed in. For three days we were confined to a small shed. At times our sense of humor wore thin. By the fourth day the weather had cleared, and the thought of facing polar bears was a relief compared with additional days of confinement.

It was bitter cold as our helicopter circled the barren tundra,

looking for signs of polar bears. "There's some tracks," Taylor shouted through the headset. Following the tracks at low altitude, we soon spotted a female bear and two yearlings. As the pilot gingerly maneuvered the helicopter, Taylor fired tranquilizer darts and sedated all three. We set down a hundred yards from the dazed bears and had about an hour to take blood and hair samples, attach a radio collar, and apply lip tattoos before they woke up. I could hardly believe that I was kneeling in the snow 200 miles from the nearest village, stroking the fur of a living polar bear.

In the 1960's biologists feared that the greatest threat to polar bears was over-hunting. Now they believe that industrial development presents a greater risk. Since bears are at the top of the marine food chain, they are the most susceptible to the contaminants like DDT, PCBs, and dioxins that are accumulating in arctic fish and mammals. Blown north with the prevailing winds from more temperate regions, these toxic substances have been found in the tissues of polar bears and whales—and in the breast milk of Inuit women in the Canadian Arctic.

In addition, wastes from mining operations are proving deadly to bears, and denning sites are being disrupted by increased transportation activity from oil and gas exploration. Biologists are also concerned that drilling for oil and gas will disrupt seal populations, eventually affecting the polar bears that feed on them.

While photographing the tagging, I noticed the female bear raising her head. It was a sign that our window of opportunity had ended. Randall and Mitch quickly packed and we dashed for the helicopter. The noise of the turbine roused the bears to their feet. We circled to check their condition and left, hoping the information contained in the samples and the ability to track their movements would help ensure their survival in this harsh land.

Another formidable creature awaited my arrival at a research site on Victoria Island. Still prehistoric in appearance, with down-turned horns, humped back, and large, powerful frame, the musk ox migrated to the Arctic from Asia via the Bering land bridge nearly 90,000 years ago. The Inuit call them "the bearded one." They have the longest hair of any mammal in North America. It protects them from cold and injury, along with their thick underfur called "quiviut," which is as warm as sheep's wool and finer than cashmere.

If threatened, musk oxen will stand their ground with a ferocity that protects them from most predators. But no amount of ferocity could protect them from the gun. Nineteenth-century hunters killed musk oxen to provision explorers and whalers and for hides to sell to fur-trading companies. By 1917 their numbers were at the brink of extinction and the Canadian government put them under protection. The arctic wolf is the only natural predator of musk oxen. Today most of Canada's musk oxen still live in the ice-free areas of the northern islands, particularly Banks, Melville, Victoria and Ellesmere. Wildlife managers continue to monitor their numbers and document their movements and habitat.

If there is one animal that epitomizes for me the open spaces and freedom of the northern wilderness, it is the caribou. Each spring, the caribou form one of the world's great wildlife migrations. From their winter homes near the Brooks Range in Alaska, the Richardson Mountains in the Yukon and the Ogilvie Mountains in the Northwest Territories, the Porcupine Caribou herd migrates to their calving grounds on the arctic coastal plain. There they fatten on the plants that grow in the short arctic summer.

The Porcupine herd, which numbers nearly 160,000 caribou, lies at the heart of one of the greatest environmental controversies in the Arctic. Much of the herd's Alaskan habitat lies within the Arctic National Wildlife Refuge (ANWR). Although development is prohibited in most of the Refuge, the calving grounds lie in an area of the coastal plain, east of Prudhoe Bay, which Congress set aside for possible oil and gas development. In addition to the caribou, millions of migratory birds from six continents use the coastal plain for nesting habitat. And the caribou have long been an integral part of the native culture, providing food, tools and clothing.

While attempts to develop the coastal plain continue, reports by the U.S. Department of the Interior, Environmental Protection Agency, and Fish and Wildlife Service have cautioned against activities that might irrevocably damage the arctic ecosystem, wildlife habitat and native community lifestyles.

Meanwhile, as they follow an ancient instinct which leads them across three mountain ranges, two provinces and one state, the home of the caribou remains one land.

MY TIME IN THE ARCTIC WAS ENDING AND AS I RODE IN A helicopter from the Anderson River back to Inuvik, the late summer sun was setting below the horizon. I now had a chance to think about all that I had seen—the people, the land, the weather, and animals. I thought about my incredible sail through the Northwest Passage. I was sad to leave, but for any great journey that ends, there is also a beginning. I know the Arctic will continue to reveal itself to me for many years to come.

A NATIVE HOMELAND

For more then a decade the Inuit of Canada have been working to create their own homeland. In 1999 the Canadian government will turn a substantial portion of the Northwest Territories into a new territory called Nunavut, meaning "our land" in Inuit. Nunavut covers about 770,000 square miles between Alaska and Baffin Island from the tree line to the North Pole.

Formed through an historic partitioning of a modern country to create a homeland for native people, Nunavut is redrafting the map of Canada. With the constitutional framework now in place, the Inuit face the long road of nation-building ahead. They will need to develop institutions that can serve far-flung communities and create a political process that will allow them to work together. It is no less difficult than the many obstacles they have faced in their long odyssey of survival and adaptation.

I saw the desire for self-determination as I traveled with hunters and visited remote communities across the Canadian Arctic. The self-reliance, resilience and resourcefulness of the Inuit in such a harsh environment was proof to me that they would succeed in any endeavor they cared deeply about.

History continues to be written by new explorers in the North American Arctic.

ACKNOWLEDGMENTS

I would like to thank my wife Christine, whose research, writing and support was instrumental to telling this story. In addition, I want to thank John Bockstoce and the crew of the *Belvedere* for a memorable journey through the Northwest Passage. I want to thank the Canadian Government and Polar Continental Shelf Project, whose involvement was crucial to the success of my National Geographic assignment. In addition, I thank Tom Selinger at the Canadian Consulate, Craig George, Randal Glaholt, Bert Dean, Dr. Mitch Taylor and countless others for their support, information, and contacts, and the U.S. and Canadian Coast Guard, whose logistical support was critical to my work. Thanks also for the design and editing skills of Bert Fox, Bill Marr and Carol Lutyk. Finally, I am deeply grateful to Bill Allen, Editor of National Geographic Magazine and Kent Kobersteen, Director of Photography, for their support of this project.

PHOTOGRAPHY BY LOCATION

MUSIC

1 · Land of the Ice Bear · (4:13)

2 · Floe-Edge · (3:13)

3 · Arctic Rain · (2:51)

4 · Nunavut (New Land) · (3:47)

5 · Shards · (4:52)

6 · Baffin Island · (3:34)

7 · Another Time · (4:12)

8 · Eider Flight · (3:07)

9 · To Approach the Land · (4:56)

10 · Ice Out · (5:02)

11 · Horizons · (4:23)

Arctic Odyssey contains both an audio CD and CD-ROM in one disc. It is playable either in a standard audio CD player or a multimedia computer (Mac or PC) which has QuickTime™ installed. To play the computer CD-ROM, deactivate any auto-player music program to avoid playing only the music portion of this disc. If you have QuickTime loaded and you see a PC alert that "Quicktime™ is not loaded," this means QT16-bit is not installed on your Window's QuickTime™ system. Simply use the QT16 installer on the disc to install it alongside QT 32. Both QT16 and QT32 can coexist on your Window's system. To get the complete QT 2.1.2™ 16 &32-bit program, go to Apple's Website at www.apple.com/quicktime.